Pocke

MW00462060

Using the NASA Form

Practical advice and tips using the NASA form when you've violated the FARs.

Darren Smith, ATP, CFII/MEI

Darren Smith, ATP, CFII/MEI
Certificated Flight Instructor
www.cfidarren.com

*"...the safety of the operator is more important than any other point.
Greater prudence is needed rather than greater skill."*
— *Wilbur Wright, 1901*

Purpose of this guide: This guide is meant to offer practical advice
and tips using the NASA form when you've violated the FARs. As a
review and reference for all pilots, it strives to present the information
to keep you current. I would love to hear from you regarding your experience with this guide. Often pilots comment about the right way,
the wrong way, and the FAA way. The result is most pilots chose the
"practical way" which is a combination of all three. I caution all pilots
to err on the side of the "safe way" so that you do not become a sta-
tistic.

Using the NASA Form (PocketLearning) / Darren Smith
ISBN-13: 978-1468096262
ISBN-10: 1468096265

Table of Contents

UPDATES TO THIS BOOK ARE FREE

www.cfidarren.com/register.htm

Protect your investment and register so that you can receive free publication updates, monthly newsletters, aviation safety notices, and free video training.

Disclaimer

I am not a lawyer.

I'm not a lawyer, I'm not giving you advice, and you should talk to a lawyer. Always seek the advice of a professional before acting on something that I might write in this publication.

Communication of information through this publication and your receipt or use of it (1) is not provided in the course of and does not create or constitute an attorney-client relationship, (2) is not a solicitation, (3) does not amount to legal advice, and (4) is not a replacement for getting legal advice from an attorney. Please do not take any actions upon any information in this publication without first seeking qualified professional counsel on your specific facts and questions.   I encourage you to base the important decision of hiring an attorney on information you obtain through your own research and interactions you have with professional counsel.

No Warranty or Liability

The information presented in this publication is provided "as is" without representation or warranty of any kind. I do not represent or warrant that the information presented herein is or will be always up-to-date, complete, or accurate.   Any representation or warranty that might be otherwise implied is expressly disclaimed.

You agree that I am not liable to you or others, in any way or for any damages of any kind or under any theory, arising from this publication, or your access to or use of or reliance on the information in this publication, including but not limited to liability or damages under contract or tort theories.

Introduction

Why do you care about the NASA form?

The NASA Form ARC 277B ("NASA Form") is a result of the Aviation Safety Reporting System, a voluntary safety reporting system established in 1975. The agreement between the FAA & NASA is meant to deficiencies in the National Aviation System. It is particularly concerned with indentifying the human factors that contribute to errors and mistakes. The hope of this NASA administrated program is that such factors could be prevented and ultimately all users of the National Aviation System benefit.

NASA Forms are available for Pilots, Air Traffic Controllers, flight attendants, mechanics, and ground personnel. As a pilot, you care about the "NASA form" because it provides you with immunity from enforcement actions by the FAA when you meet certain requirements.

If you bust airspace, blow an altitude or restriction, or unintentionally break a FAR, you can report it to a neutral 3rd party (NASA) in the hopes that others can learn from your mistake. The FAA feels this is a constructive attitude towards preventing further mistakes and errors. Therefore, the FAA has committed not to use such reports against participants in enforcement actions. It also has agreed to waive fines and penalties, subject to certain limitations, for unintentional violations of federal aviation statutes and regulations when they are reported using the NASA form.

Are There Exceptions?

You bet. There are some limited exceptions:

O   If you intended to violate the rules, you don't get the benefit of the safety program.

O   If the violation was criminal in nature, you can't participate in the safety program.

O   If you have been cited of a FAR violation in the preceding five years - you can participate in the safety program, but you will not receive immunity for your actions when it comes to certificate actions.

O   You must submit your report within 10 days of the incident, or when you became aware, or should reasonably have become aware that an incident or violation occurred.

O   If the incident resulted in death, serious injury or substantial aircraft damage, you are not likely covered by the safety program. Some incidents (not accidents) are not considered serious to the FAA. Always discuss the specifics of your incident/violation with an attorney.

O   If the you are exercising privileges of a certificate you do not hold, you are not likely to benefit from the safety program. Again, contact an attorney to discuss the specifics of your case.

Why You Should Keep a Supply of These

Some airline pilots submit dozens of these safety notices (or their equivalent, the ASAP program) over their career. Even the most experienced among us, who are out in the airspace everyday can run afoul of rules and regulations that are growing in complexity and changing everyday. How much more trouble does the occasional pilot subject himself to when he flies?

Keep a stock of these forms so you can record the pertinent details when the incident occurs.

Why You Should Participate

Well the most important reason is to protect the certificate you worked so hard to obtain. Your report can keep you out of trouble when it comes to certificate action. The second most important reason is somewhat altruistic. You want to make our National Aviation System the best it can be. That means identifying its weaknesses for the benefit of all.

In any case, you can't be penalized for participating. There's only an up-side to participating.

If I haven't impressed this point on you yet, be sure to discuss the specifics of your case with an attorney. There are many aviation legal programs available that can help you get a consult for a very reasonable price. Always be careful with what you write as the English language is significantly complex that the choice of a single word could cause your report to be excluded from the program (accidental versus intentional, for example).

Submit your report online:

http://asrs.arc.nasa.gov/report/electronic.html

The Official Briefing Direct from NASA

Topics:
Program Briefing
Confidentiality and Incentives to Report
Immunity Policy
FAR 91.25
Report Processing
Important Points to Remember

Program Briefing

Summary

The ASRS is a small but important facet of the continuing effort by government, industry, and individuals to maintain and improve aviation safety. The ASRS collects voluntarily submitted aviation safety incident/situation reports from pilots, controllers, and others.

The ASRS acts on the information these reports contain. It identifies system deficiencies, and issues alerting messages to persons in a position to correct them. It educates through its newsletter CALLBACK, its journal ASRS Directline and through its research studies. Its database is a public repository which serves the FAA and NASA's needs and those of other organizations world-wide which are engaged in research and the promotion of safe flight.

Purpose

The ASRS collects, analyzes, and responds to voluntarily submitted aviation safety incident reports in order to lessen the likelihood of aviation accidents.

ASRS data are used to:
O Identify deficiencies and discrepancies in the National Aviation System (NAS) so that these can be remedied by appropriate authorities.
O Support policy formulation and planning for, and improvements to, the NAS.
O Strengthen the foundation of aviation human factors safety research. This is particularly important since it is generally conceded that over two-thirds of all aviation accidents and incidents have their roots in human performance errors.

The ASRS Staff

The ASRS Staff is composed of highly experienced pilots, air traffic controllers and mechanics, as well as a management team that possess aviation and human factors experience. ASRS Analysts' experience is comprised of over 200 cumulative years of aviation expertise covering the full spectrum of aviation activity: air carrier, corporate, military, and general aviation; Air Traffic Control in Towers, TRACONs, Centers, and Military Facilities. Analyst cumulative flight time exceeds 100,000 hours in over 50 different aircraft.

ASRS Analysts' first mission is to identify any aviation hazards that are discussed in reports and flag that information for immediate action. When such hazards are identified, an alerting message is issued to the appropriate FAA office or aviation authority. Their second mission is to classify reports and diagnose the causes underlying each reported event.

In addition, the ASRS Staff has human factors and psychology research experience in areas such as crew resource management, training, fatigue, user interface design, usability evaluations, and research methodology.

Confidentiality and Incentives to Report

Pilots, air traffic controllers, flight attendants, mechanics, ground personnel, and others involved in aviation operations submit reports to the ASRS when they are involved in, or observe, an incident or situation in which aviation safety may have been compromised. All submissions are voluntary.

Reports sent to the ASRS are held in strict confidence. More than 880,000 reports have been submitted to date and no reporter's identity has ever been breached by the ASRS. ASRS de-identifies reports before entering them into the incident database. All personal and organizational names are removed. Dates, times, and related information, which could be used to infer an identity, are either generalized or eliminated.

The FAA offers ASRS reporters further guarantees and incentives to report. It has committed itself not to use ASRS information against reporters in enforcement actions. It has also chosen to waive fines and penalties, subject to certain limitations, for unintentional violations of federal aviation statutes and regulations which are reported to ASRS. The FAA's initiation, and continued support of the ASRS program and its willingness to waive penalties in qualifying cases is a measure of the value it places on the safety information gathered, and the products made possible, through incident reporting to the ASRS.

How Soon Should You Report?

Although a finding of violation may be made, neither a civil penalty nor certificate suspension will be imposed if the person proves that, **within 10 days** after the violation, or when you became aware of the violation, he or she completed and delivered or mailed a written report of the incident or occurrence to NASA under ASRS.

Immunity Policy

The following is an excerpt of Advisory Circular 00-46E:

4. NASA Responsibilities
O   NASA ASRS provides for the receipt, analysis, and de-
    identification of aviation safety reports; in addition, periodic
    reports of findings obtained through the reporting program are
    published and distributed to the public, the aviation commu-
    nity, and the FAA.
O   A NASA ASRS Advisory Subcommittee, composed of repre-
    sentatives from the aviation community, including the Depart-
    ment of Defense, NASA, and FAA, advises NASA on the con-
    duct of the ASRS. The subcommittee conducts periodic meet-
    ings to evaluate and ensure the effectiveness of the reporting
    system.

5. Prohibition Against the Use of Reports for Enforcement Purposes
A. Section 91.25 of the Federal Aviation Regulations (FAR) (14
    CFR 91.25) prohibits the use of any reports submitted to
    NASA under the ASRS (or information derived therefrom) in
    any disciplinary action, except information concerning criminal
    offenses or accidents which are covered under paragraphs 7a
    and b.

B. When violation of the FAR comes to the attention of the FAA
    from a source other than a report filed with NASA under the
    ASRS, appropriate action will be taken. See paragraph 9.

C. The NASA ASRS security system is designed and operated by
    NASA to ensure confidentiality and anonymity of the reporter
    and all other parties involved in a reported occurrence or inci-
    dent. The FAA will not seek, and NASA will not release or
    make available to the FAA, any report filed with NASA under
    the ASRS or any other information that might reveal the iden-
    tity of any party involved in an occurrence or incident reported
    under the ASRS. There has been no breach of confidentiality
    in more than 30 years of the ASRS under NASA management.

6. Reporting Procedures
Forms in the NASA ARC 277 series have been prepared specifi-
cally for intended users (including ARC 277A for air traffic use,
277B for general use including pilots, 277C for flight attendants
and 277D for maintenance personnel) and are preaddressed and
postage free. Completed forms or a narrative report should be
completed and mailed only to ASRS at NASA, Aviation Safety Reporting System, P.O. Box 189, Moffett Field, CA 94035-9800.

7. Processing of Reports
NASA procedures for processing Aviation Safety Reports ensure
that the reports are initially screened for:

A. Information concerning criminal offenses, which will be re-
    ferred promptly to the Department of Justice and the FAA;

B. information concerning accidents, which will be referred
    promptly to the National Transportation Safety Board (NTSB)
    and the FAA; and

    Note: Reports discussing criminal activities or accidents are
    not de-identified prior to their referral to the agencies outlined
    above.

C. time-critical information which, after de-identification, will be
    promptly referred to the FAA and other interested parties.

Each Aviation Safety Report has a tear-off portion which contains
the information that identifies the person submitting the report.
This tear-off portion will be removed by NASA, time stamped, and
returned to the reporter as a receipt. This will provide the reporter
with proof that he/she filed a report on a specific incident or occurrence. The identification strip section of the ASRS report form provides NASA program personnel with the means by which the reporter can be contacted in case additional information is sought in
order to understand more completely the report's content Except
in the case of reports describing accidents or criminal activities, no
copy of an ASRS form's identification strip is created or retained
for ASRS files. Prompt return of identification strips is a primary
element of the ASRS program's report de-identification process
and ensures the reporter's anonymity.

8. De-Identification

All information that might assist in or establish the identification of persons filing ASRS reports and parties named in those reports will be deleted, except for reports covered under paragraphs 7a and 7b. This de-identification will be accomplished normally within 72 hours after NASA's receipt of the reports, if no further information is requested from the reporter.

9. Enforcement Policy

The Administrator of the FAA will perform his/her responsibility under Title 49, United States Code, Subtitle VII, and enforce the statute and the FAR in a manner that will reduce or eliminate the possibility of, or recurrence of, aircraft accidents. The FAA enforcement procedures are set forth in Part 13 of the FAR (14 CFR Part 13) and FAA enforcement handbooks.

In determining the type and extent of the enforcement action to be taken in a particular case, the following factors are considered:
1. nature of the violation;
2. whether the violation was inadvertent or deliberate;
3. the certificate holder's level of experience and responsibility;
4. attitude of the violator;
5. the hazard to safety of others which should have been foreseen;
6. action taken by employer or other government authority;
7. length of time which has elapsed since violation;(8) the certificate holder's use of the certificate;
8. the need for special deterrent action in a particular regulatory area, or segment of the aviation community; and
9. presence of any factors involving national interest, such as the use of aircraft for criminal purposes.

The filing of a report with NASA concerning an incident or occurrence involving a violation of 49 U.S.C. Subtitle VII, or the FAR is considered by FAA to be indicative of a constructive attitude. Such an attitude will tend to prevent future violations. Accordingly, although a finding of violation may be made, neither a civil penalty nor certificate suspension will be imposed if:
O the violation was inadvertent and not deliberate;
O the violation did not involve a criminal offense, or accident. or

action under 49 U.S.C. Section 44709 which discloses a lack
of qualification or competency, which is wholly excluded from
this policy;

○ the person has not been found in any prior FAA enforcement
action to have committed a violation of 49 U.S.C. Subtitle VII,
or any regulation promulgated there for a period of **5 years**
prior to the date of occurrence; and

○ the person proves that, within **10 days** after the violation, or
when the individual became aware, or should reasonably have
become aware that an incident or violation occurred he or she
completed and delivered or mailed a written report of the incident or occurrence to NASA under ASRS. See paragraphs 5c
and 7b.

Report Processing

Incident reports are read and analyzed by ASRS's corps of aviation safety analysts. The analyst staff is composed entirely of experienced pilots, air traffic controllers, and mechanics. Their years
of experience are uniformly measured in decades, and cover the
full spectrum of aviation activity: air carrier, military, and general
aviation; Air Traffic Control in Towers, TRACONs, Centers, and
Military Facilities.

Each report received by the ASRS is read by a minimum of two
analysts. Their first mission is to identify any aviation hazards
which are discussed in reports and flag that information for immediate action. When such hazards are identified, an alerting message is issued to the appropriate FAA office or aviation authority.
Analysts' second mission is to classify reports and diagnose the
causes underlying each reported event. Their observations, and
the original de-identified report, are then incorporated into the
ASRS's database.

FAR 91.25

Prohibition Against Use of Report for Enforcement Purposes
The Administrator of the FAA will not use reports submitted to the National Aeronautics and Space Administration under the Aviation Safety Reporting Program (or information derived therefrom) in any enforcement action, except information concerning accidents or criminal offenses which are wholly excluded from the program.

Important Things to Remember

The ASRS assurance of confidentiality and the availability of waivers of disciplinary action do NOT extend to reports of accidents or criminal activity (e.g., hijacking, bomb threats, and drug running). Such reports should not be submitted to ASRS. If such reports are received, they are forwarded identified to cognizant agencies.

FAA policies regarding the ASRS are covered by Advisory Circular 00-46D and FAR 91.25. The waiver of penalties is subject to the following limitations: (A) the alleged violation must be inadvertent and not deliberate, (B) it must not reveal an event subject to Section 609 of the Federal Aviation Act, (C) the reporter must not have been found guilty of a violation of the FARs or the Federal Aviation Act during the preceding five years, and (D) the ASRS report must be submitted within 10 days of the event.

The ASRS professional staff is composed of retired controllers, mechanics, as well as both active and retired pilots. To avoid conflicts of interest, ASRS analysts, researchers, and management personnel are not permitted to have ongoing employment relationships with the FAA, air carriers, or similar organizations.

ASRS's mailing address is:
P.O. Box 189
Moffett Field, California, 94035-0189.

Consider the electronically submitting your report (preferred method):
http://asrs.arc.nasa.gov/report/electronic.html

Confidentiality

Reports sent to the ASRS are held in strict confidence. More than 850,000 reports have been submitted (through October, 2009) and no reporter's identity has ever been breached by the ASRS. ASRS de-identifies reports before entering them into the incident database. All personal and organizational names are removed. Dates, times, and related information, which could be used to infer an identity, are either generalized or eliminated.

De-identification of reporting form fixed and text fields is conducted as a normal part of report coding by aviation expert analysts. A standard set of rules for de-identification is employed, however, when the nature of an incident or operation is such that standard de-identification may not be sufficient to ensure reporter anonymity, a special set of rules are employed.

Note: ASRS uses "ZZZ," if required, to de-identify fields normally expected to contain a discrete value (such as location). If the information is unknown (as opposed to de-identified) the field will be left blank.

What Researchers Know About Your Report

ASRS reports referencing safety incidents are considered soft data. The reports are submitted voluntarily and are subject to self-reporting biases. Such incidents, in many cases, have not been corroborated by the FAA or NTSB. The existence in the ASRS database of records concerning a specific topic cannot, therefore, be used to infer the prevalence of that problem within the National Airspace System.

Reports submitted to ASRS may be amplified by contact with the individual who submitted them, but the information provided by the reporter is not investigated further. At best, it represents the perception of a specific individual involved in or witnessing a given issue or event.

Your Report Could Help Others

Consider the following table. This data lists the categories and numbers of reports that were considered safety alerts and were referred to appropriate officials and what happened.

January 1999 – December 2009

Subject	Total
Aircraft Systems	891
Airport Facility Status and Maintenance	450
ATC Operations	322
Other	222
Airport Lighting and Approach Aids	153
ATC Procedures	146
Hazards to Flight	128
ATC Equipment	118
Aircraft Powerplants	114
Navigation	70
Aircraft Avionics	56

January 1999 – December 2009

Response	Percentage
Action taken as a result of the AB/FYI	28%
Action initiated in response to AB/FYI but not completed	12%
Action initiated before AB/FYI was received	11%
Issue raised by AB/FYI under investigation	6%
Addressee in factual agreement but sees no problem	6%
Addressee agrees with AB/FYI but is unable to resolve	3%

Should I Submit My Report Online?

Absolutely. Both paper report (see download link next page) and electronic submission are available to users of the safety program.

By submitting an electronic report, you completely avoid the "lost in the mail" problem. There is also benefit to the NASA program which services the safety program: cost. As of this writing, the safety program has not received a budget increase since 1997. This is the preferred method for speed, accuracy, and cost.

Some might think of doing both. While this is inadvisable, some are still going to try it. If you do, please write at the top of your narrative something like:
> *"This is a hard copy follow-up to the electronic version submitted on _____(date)."*

To access either option, see the following links:

Submit your report online:
http://asrs.arc.nasa.gov/report/electronic.html

Download the latest form:
www.cfidarren.com/nasa.pdf

Step by Step: The Form

(SPACE BELOW RESERVED FOR ASRS DATE/TIME STAMP)

IDENTIFICATION STRIP: *Please fill in all blanks to ensure return of strip.*
NO RECORD WILL BE KEPT OF YOUR IDENTITY. This section will be returned to you.

TELEPHONE NUMBERS where we may reach you for further
details of this occurrence:

HOME   Area _____ No. _____   Hours _____

WORK   Area _____ No. _____   Hours _____

NAME _____

ADDRESS/PO BOX _____

_____

CITY _____ STATE ____ ZIP _____

TYPE OF EVENT/SITUATION

_____

_____

DATE OF OCCURRENCE _____
(MM/DD/YYYY)
LOCAL TIME (24 hr. clock) _____
(HH:MM)

PLEASE FILL IN APPROPRIATE SPACES AND CHECK ALL ITEMS WHICH APPLY TO THIS EVENT OR SITUATION.

Identification Strip

This top part of the form will be returned to you after it has been stamped with the NASA ASRS time/date stamp. These details will not be logged by NASA. The primary use of the Identification Strip is so that should you encounter FAA certificate action, you would produce this receipt to prove you had filed the report. The FAA can use this information to look at your anonymous report.

It doesn't work the other way around however. The FAA can't search the NASA forms to find this information because NASA never records this data with your anonymous report.

Note that NASA does retain the report year/month and general time period in their database. The time of your incident (local time) is stored by NASA as one of these time bands:
O   0001-0600
O   0601-1200
O   1201-1800
O   1801-2400

You can be sure that even the specific time & date of your incident is not saved by NASA. You may be contacted by a NASA data analyst if they need to clarify elements of your report. This will be done before the Identification strip is returned to you

A Word About Report Title

There had been controversy about the report title. It was widely reported that the report title given on the "Type of Event/ Situation" lines is not confidential.

There has been significant interaction between the FAA and the Administrative Law Judge (ALJ) which started the controversy with a creative legal opinion. This has resolved the concern, and is not considered a problem going forward.

There are ways to word your title in a way that doesn't admit to a FAR violation. Here are some examples of ambiguous titles:

○ *Situational awareness—surface movement*
    instead of runway incursion
○ *Situational awareness—navigation*
    instead of violating Class B

As you write the rest of your report, it is important that you be as clear as possible with the details surrounding your event.

Reporter

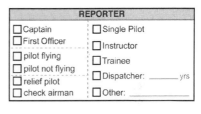

The left column is primarily for Part 135/121 operations. Most General Aviation pilots will not select from the left column. If you were alone the check **Single Pilot**.

If this was a training flight, the instructor would check **Instructor** and the student would check **Trainee**. This doesn't correlate to how you log PIC time in your logbook.

If you are conducting safety pilot operations and both are logging the time, both pilots should seek the protection of filing a NASA form since both are logging the time. In the case of safety pilot operations, the pilot under the hood is **pilot flying** and the safety pilot is the **pilot not flying**.

Flying Time

FLYING TIME (in hours)	
Total Time	_____ hrs
Last 90 Days	_____ hrs
Time in Type	_____ hrs

Report your flying time in rounded whole hours. For total time, it includes all kinds of flying time, solo or not, PIC or not, etc. Last 90 days refers to your most recent total time.
Time in type refers to the specific model of aircraft, such as Cessna 172 (all models including RG), PA28 (all models), etc. You can see the typical aircraft types used in Personal and Training flights in the Reference section of this book.

Certificates & Ratings

CERTIFICATES & RATINGS	
☐ Student	☐ Flight Instructor
☐ Sport/Rec	☐ Multiengine
☐ Private	☐ Instrument
☐ Commercial	☐ Flight Engineer
☐ ATP	☐ Other: _____

Put a check next to your highest certificate held—check only one certificate from the left column. From the right column, put a check next to all that apply.

ATC Experience

ATC EXPERIENCE	
☐ FPL ☐ Developmental	
radar	_____ yrs
non-radar	_____ yrs
supervisory	_____ yrs
military	_____ yrs

This is not applicable to pilots.

Airspace

AIRSPACE	
☐ Class A	☐ Class E
☐ Class B	☐ Class G
☐ Class C	☐ Special Use
☐ Class D	☐ TFR

Put a check by the airspace you were in. Check only one.

Conditions/ Weather Elements

CONDITIONS / WEATHER ELEMENTS		
☐ VMC	☐ fog	☐ snow
☐ IMC	☐ hail	☐ thunderstorm
	☐ haze/smoke	☐ turbulence
☐ Mixed	☐ icing	☐ windshear
☐ Marginal	☐ rain	☐ other: _____

From the first column, select the conditions: VMC, IMC, Mixed or Marginal. Marginal is defined as visibilities between 1 and 3 NM. From the other two columns, select any other weather elements present during the flight.

Light/Visibility

LIGHT / VISIBILITY	
☐ dawn	☐ night
☐ daylight	☐ dusk
Ceiling _____ feet	
Visibility _____ miles	
RVR _____ feet	

Select the appropriate conditions for your flight. To use RVR, you must have been at an airport reporting Runway Visual Range (RVR).

ATC/Advisory SVC

ATC / ADVISORY SVC.	
☐ Ramp	☐ Center
☐ Ground	☐ FSS
☐ Tower	☐ UNICOM
☐ TRACON	☐ CTAF
ATC Facility Name: _____	

This data box asks you to consider what your primary COM radio was tuned to. Check the appropriate box and then select the appropriate facility name. Examples:

Ramp—KJFK   Ground—KDCA
Tower—KMIA   TRACON—TPA
UNICOM—KPIE CTAF—KOCF
Center—ZFW (Fort Worth Center)

A word about FSS: Lockheed Martin Flight Services operates three large 24-hour FSS hubs, one 24-hour satellite facility and two part-time satellite facilities. LMFS facilities are interconnected so as to provide continuous services at all locations, and provide backup if a site were to go down. Alaska FAA FSS facilities operate three 24-hour hub facilities and fourteen part-time and seasonal satellite facilities. You may not be able to list the FSS facility as you could in the old days.

AIRCRAFT 1		
Your Aircraft Type (Make/Model) (e.g. B737) NOT "N #", Flt #, etc.: _____		**Operating FAR Part:** _____
Operator	☐ air carrier ☐ air taxi ☐ corporate	☐ fractional ☐ FBO ☐ government	☐ military ☐ personal ☐ other: _____
Mission	☐ passenger ☐ personal	☐ cargo/freight ☐ training	☐ ferry ☐ other: _____
Flight Plan	☐ VFR ☐ IFR	☐ SVFR ☐ DVFR	☐ none
Flight Phase	☐ taxi ☐ parked ☐ takeoff ☐ initial climb	☐ climb ☐ cruise ☐ descent ☐ initial approach	☐ final approach ☐ missed/GAR ☐ landing ☐ other: _____
Route in Use	☐ airway (ID): _____ ☐ direct ☐ SID (ID): _____	☐ STAR (ID): _____ ☐ oceanic ☐ vectors	☐ visual approach ☐ none ☐ other: _____

Aircraft Type

For the most part, any FAA approved aircraft type will be accepted here. For simplicity's sake, the NASA data analyst will use the aircraft types listed in the *Reference* Chapter of this book.

Operating FAR Part

For the most part, you will write 91 here unless you conducting air carrier, air taxi, or charter operations.

Operator

Most General Aviation users are going to select personal unless one of the other categories applies to your situation. If you were conducting FBO business, check it.

Mission

Most General Aviation users are going to select personal or training (with a CFI). There are some situations where a ferry permit was issued and you might select that. And if you were conducting air carrier/air taxi operations, you would select passenger or cargo/freight.

Flight Plan

Select the flight plan type that you were using, if any. If you had an open VFR flight plan with FSS, if you didn't, select none. DVFR would be selected if you were on a flight plan with ATC crossing an ADIZ.

Flight Phase

Self explanatory, but here are some industry definitions which can help you decide:

Phase	Trigger/Starts With	Ends With
1. Parked	Walking out to the aircraft.	After start checklist
2. Taxi/Takeoff	Movement for the purpose of flight	Breaking ground
3. Departure (Climb)	Aircraft departs the runway	Top of the enroute climb
4. Enroute Cruise	Level off at altitude	Top of descent
5. Descent	Instruction to descend from cruise	ATC approach clearance
6. Approach	ATC approach clearance	Runway in sight, stabilized position to land
7. Landing	Runway in sight, stabilized position to land	Clearing the runway, after landing checks
8. Taxi/Shutdown	Movement for the purpose to park the aircraft	Aircraft is secured

Some of these steps are broken down further on the NASA form such as step 2 could be either **taxi** or **takeoff** while step 8 could be either **taxi** or **parked**. Step 3 could be **initial climb** (i.e. before the cowl flaps are closed and climb power set) or **climb** (when the climb checklist is completed to the top of the enroute altitude). So use your best judgment to indicate the phase of flight the incident occurred during.

Route in Use

If you were using any ATC assigned routing, list it here. It is unlikely you would be using a **STAR, SID, oceanic, vectors,** or **visual approach** without being under ATC control.

For VFR users without ATC control, you are most likely using a GPS, so choose the **direct** option. If you were using an **airway** under VFR conditions, list it.

Other Aircraft/Aircraft 2
If there was another aircraft involved (such as a near-miss), list everything you can determine as it relates to the other aircraft. If there were additional aircraft, list all the pertinent details of additional aircraft in your narrative.

Location

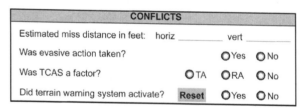

LOCATION			
Altitude: _____ (single value)	☐MSL ☐AGL		
Distance: _____ and/or Radial (bearing): _____ from:			
☐Airport _____	☐ATC Fac _____		
☐Intersection _____	☐NAVAID _____		

If you were at an airport, intersection, or NAVAID, select 0NM and list it. A radial is not needed. The best location for the report is the nearest position to any airport, intersection, or NAVAID. Example: 10NM—030 radial—PIE VOR.

Conflicts

CONFLICTS			
Estimated miss distance in feet: horiz _____ vert _____			
Was evasive action taken?		○Yes	○No
Was TCAS a factor?	○TA	○RA	○No
Did terrain warning system activate?	Reset	○Yes	○No

In the case of near mid-air collision, it is helpful for you to estimate the miss distance in horizontal miles and vertical feet.

Most General Aviation users are unlikely to have TCAS or terrain warning systems installed and these questions can be ignored.

Narrative

The last remaining area of the NASA form is the Narrative section. Please write your report legibly, in black ink, so the NASA data analyst can easily read and transcribe your report. It is useful to avoid acronyms altogether, but if you do, there are some that NASA does recognize. There are 6 pages of them in the *Reference* chapter of this book.

The following are general tips on writing the narrative of your report. I must stress the importance of complete honesty in your reporting. The narrative section is where you lay all your cards on the table. This is where you take the opportunity of your error to describe the mistake you made and save other pilots from making it too.

You can't be penalized for what is written here, except in two specific circumstances:

O The report is about an aircraft accident. Those are not included in the NASA safety program, therefore you should not file a NASA report.

O There was criminal activity of any kind. This could include violating a TFR, if your acts were intentional and the TFR was for national security or VIP protection.

If you have any doubt, contact an attorney to review the circumstances of your specific case.

It is not required, but extremely helpful to NASA personnel if you would indicate at the beginning of your narrative if there was a crew of 2 or more individuals operating the aircraft. This is typically going to be a corporate, fractional, air carrier, air taxi, government, or military operator <u>AND</u> the aircraft would require a crew of 2 or more individuals to operate it. Be sure to include whether you were Captain or First Officer in the **Reporter** box if this applies. Then make it clear in your narrative: just write a short sentence at the top of your narrative:

Flight crew of 2 individuals.

Malfunctions, Failures, Incorrect Operation

If there was any aircraft component problem, it would be very helpful to NASA personnel if you would list it at the very top of your narrative. Examples:

Aircraft component malfunction: Airspeed Indicator
Aircraft component failure: vacuum pump powering attitude indicator
Aircraft component incorrectly operated: pitot-static anti ice

The following is a list of commonly used aircraft components which have malfunctioned and became a factor in a NASA report:

AC Generation
AC Generation Indicating and Warning
AC Generator/Alternator
ADF
Aero Charts
Aerofoil Ice System
Aeroplane Flight Control
AHRS/ND
Aileron
Aileron Control System
Air Conditioning and Pressurization Pack
Air Conditioning Compressor
Air Conditioning Distribution Ducting,
        Clamps, Connectors
Air/Ground Communication
Aircraft Component
Aircraft Documentation
Aircraft Furnishing
Aircraft Heating System
Aircraft Logbook(s)
Airspeed Indicator
Altimeter
Altitude Alert
Altitude Hold/Capture
Approach Coupler
Attitude Indicator (Gyro/Horizon/ADI)
Autoflight System
Autoflight Yaw Damper
Autopilot
Brake System
Cabin Window
Camshaft
Carburetor
Carburetor Heat Control
Cargo Door
Cargo/Baggage
Checklists
Chip Detector
Circuit Breaker / Fuse / Thermocouple
Cockpit Canopy Window
Cockpit Door
Cockpit Furnishing

Cockpit Lighting
Cockpit Window
Collective Control
Combustor Assembly
Communication Systems
Compass (HSI/ETC)
Component
Cowl Flap
Cowling
Cowling/Nacelle Fasteners, Latches
Crankcase
Cylinder
Cylinder Head
Cylinder Head Temperature
DC Battery
DC Generation
DC Generator
DC Regulator
Door
Door Warning System
Electrical Distribution
Electrical Power
Electrical Wiring & Connectors
Electrical/Electronic Panel & Parts
Electronic Flt Bag (EFB)
Elevator
Elevator Control Column
Elevator Control System
Elevator Trim System
Emergency Extension System
Engine
Engine Air
Engine Analyzers
Engine Control
Engine Cranking
Engine Driven Pump
Engine Electric Starter
Engine Fuel Filter
Engine Indications
Engine Oil Seals
Engine Starting System
Exhaust Manifold

I've Screwed Up! Now What? - Using the NASA Form

Exhaust Pipe
Exhaust Turbo Charger
Exterior Pax/Crew Door
External Power
FADEC / TCC
FCC (Flight Control Computer)
FCU (Flight Control Unit)
Filter
Fire/Overheat Warning
Flap Control (Trailing & Leading Edge)
Flap Vane
Flap/Slat Control System
Flap/Slat Indication
Flight Director
Flight Dynamics
Flight Dynamics Navigation and Safety
FMS/FMC
Fuel
Fuel Booster Pump
Fuel Contents Indication
Fuel Crossfeed
Fuel Distribution System
Fuel Drain
Fuel Flow Indication
Fuel Line, Fittings, & Connectors
Fuel Quantity-Pressure Indication
Fuel Selector
Fuel Storage System
Fuel System
Fuel Tank
Fuel Tank Cap
Fuselage Panel
Gear Down Lock
Gear Extend/Retract Mechanism
Gear Float
Gear Lever/Selector
Gear Up Lock
Generator Drive Indicators & Warning System
GPS & Other Satellite Navigation
GPWS
Headset
Horizontal Stabilizer Control
Horizontal Stabilizer Trim
Hydraulic Main System
Hydraulic System
Hydraulic Lines, Connectors, Fittings
Ice/Rain Protection System
Igniter Plug
Ignition/Magneto Switch
ILS/VOR
Indicating and Warning Flight / Navigation
Indicating and Warning - Fuel System

Indicating and Warning - Landing Gear
Injector
Intake Alternate Air Valve
Intake Assembly
Intake Ice System
Integrated Audio System
Interphone System
Landing Gear
Landing Gear Indicating System
Landing Light
Loran
Lubrication Oil
Magneto/Distributor
Main Gear
Main Gear Tire
Main Gear Wheel
Main Rotor RPM Indication
MCP
Microphone
Nacelle/Pylon Skin
Navigation Database
Navigational Equipment and Processing
Normal Brake System
Nose Gear
Nose Gear Door
Nose Gear Tire
Nose Gear Wheel
Nosewheel Steering
Oil Cooler
Oil Distribution
Oil Filler Cap
Oil Filter
Oil Line
Oil Pressure Indication
Oil Pump
Oil Storage
Oxygen System/Crew
Parking Brake
PFD
Pilot Seat
Piston
Pitot/Static Ice System
Pitot-Static System
Pneumatic System
Pneumatic System Control
Pneumatic Valve/Bleed Valve
Positional / Directional Sensing
Powerplant Fuel Control
Powerplant Fuel System
Powerplant Fuel Valve
Powerplant Lubrication System
Powerplant Mounting
Pressurization Control System

Pressurization System
Propeller
Propeller Assembly
Propeller Blade
Propeller Control
Propeller Ice System
Propeller Pitch Change Mechanism
Propeller Spinner
Radio Altimeter
Reciprocating Engine Assembly
RPM/N1/N2/Etc Indication
Rudder
Rudder Control System
Rudder Pedal
Rudder Trim System
Seatbelt
Service/Access Door
Spark Plug
Spoiler System
Stall Warning System
Supplemental Landing Gear
Switch
System Monitor: Indicating and Warning
Tail Boom

Tail Rotor
Tail Wheel
TCAS Equipment
Throttle/Power Level
Thrust Reverser Control
Tires
Traffic Collision Avoidance System (TCAS)
Trailing Edge Flap
Transponder
Turbine Engine
Turbine Inlet Temperature Indication
UHF
Vacuum Pump
Vacuum System
Valve/Oil System
VHF
Wheel Assemblies
Wheels/Tires/Brakes
Wing
Wing Attachment
Wing Fairing
Wing Leading Edge
Wing Strut
Wingtip

Human Factors

If you feel that there were human factors concerns that affected or caused the incident, it would be very helpful to the NASA data analysts if you would list those at the top of the report narrative. Example:

Human factors concern—communications breakdown with ATC

Here's a list of those concerns that NASA has the most experience with. Feel free to list any of these as part of your report narrative if applicable.

Communication Breakdown
Distraction
Human Factors
Physiological - Other
Time Pressure
Troubleshooting

Confusion
Fatigue
Human-Machine Interface
Situational Awareness
Training / Qualification
Workload

Do not be shy about listing these human factors (or others) if it is applicable to your report.

"I learned that danger is relative, and that experience can be a magnifying glass."
— Charles A. Lindbergh (1902-1974)

Reference

Topics:
Acronyms According to NASA
Aircraft Types According to NASA

Acronyms According to NASA

AC - Alternating Current
ACARS - Automatic Communications Addressing & Reporting System
ACFT - Aircraft
ACR - Air Carrier
ADC - Air Data Computer
ADF - Automatic Direction Finder
ADG - Air Driven Generator
ADI - Attitude Direction Indicator
ADIZ - Air Defense Identification Zone
AERO - Aeronautical
AFB - Air Force Base
AFD - Airport/Facility Directory
AFDS - Autopilot and Flight Director System
AFSS - Automated Flight Service Station
AGL - Above Ground Level
AIM - Aeronautical Information Manual
ALS - Automatic Landing System
ALSF-1 - Standard 2400' Hi-Intensity Approach Lighting System With Sequenced Flashers (Cat I Config)
ALSF-2 - Standard 2400' Hi-Intensity Approach Lighting System With Sequenced Flashers (Cat II Config)
ALT(S) - Altitude
ALTDEV - Altitude Deviation
AM - Ante Meridiem
AMB - Ambiguity
AME - Aviation Medical Examiner
ANG - Air National Guard
APCH (S, ED, ING) - Approach
APCH CTL - Approach Control
APPROX - Approximately
APU - Auxiliary Power Unit
ARPT(S) - Airport
ARR - Arrival, Arrive
ARSR - Air Route Surveillance Radar
ARTCC - Air Route Traffic Control Center
ARTS - Automated Radar Terminal Systems
ASAP - As Soon As Possible
ASOS - Automated Surface Observation System
ASR - Airport Surveillance Radar
ASRS - Aviation Safety Reporting System
ATA - Actual Time Of Arrival
ATA - Air Traffic Area
ATC - Air Traffic Control
ATCT - Airport Traffic Control Tower

ATD - Actual Time Of Departure
ATIS - Automatic Terminal Information Service
ATOG - Allowable Takeoff Gross Weight
ATP - Airline Transport Pilot Certificate
ATR - Airline Transport Rating
ATTN - Attention
AUTH - Authority/Authorized
AUTO - Automatic
AUX - Auxiliary
AVG - Average
AVGAS - Aviation Gasoline
AWOS - Automatic Weather Observing System
BAL (S, ED, ING) - Balance
BASE OPS - Base Operations Office
BC - Back Course
BCSTN - Broadcast Station
BFR - Biennial Flight Review
BKN - Broken
BRITE - Bright Radar Indicator Tower Equipment
BTWN - Between
C - Celsius
CAB - Cabin Attendant
CADC - Central Air Data Computer
CAP - Civil Air Patrol
CAPT - Captain
CARB - Carburetor
CAT - Category
CAT - Clear Air Turbulence
CAWS - Central Aural Warning System
CB - Circuit Breaker
CD - Clearance Delivery
CDI - Course Deviation Indicator
CDT - Central Daylight Time
CDU - Control Display Unit
CFI - Certificated Flight Instructor
CFIT - Controlled Flight Into Terrain
CFR - Crash Fire Rescue Equipment
CGP - Company Ground Personnel
CHK (S, ED, ING) - Check
CIC - Controller In Charge
CLB (S, ED, ING) - Climb
CLR (S, ED, ING) - Clear
CLRNC - Clearance
COM(S) - Communication
CONFIG - Configuration
COORD - Coordination
CPU - Central Processing Unit

I've Screwed Up! Now What? - Using the NASA Form

CRM - Cockpit Resource Management
CRT - Cathode Ray Tube
CSD - Constant Speed Drive
CST - Central Standard Time
CTAF - Common Traffic Advisory Frequency
CTL (S, ED, ING) - Control
CTLR (S,'S) - Controller
CTR - Center
DB - Decibel
DCU - Data Control Unit
DEG(S) - Degree
DEMO - Demonstration
DEP(S) - Departure
DEPT(S) - Department
DEST(S) - Destination
DEV(S) - Deviation
DF - Direction Finder
DFDR - Digital Flight Data Recorder
DFGS - Digital Flight Guidance System
DGPS - Differential Global Positioning System
DH - Decision Height
DISTR - Distraction
DME - Distance Measuring Equipment
DOD - Department Of Defense
DOE - Department Of Energy
DOT - Department Of Transportation
DSCNT - Descent
DSND (S, ED, ING) - Descend
DVFR - Defense Visual Flight Rules
EAC - Expected Approach Clearance
EAT - Expected Approach Time
EBND - Eastbound
ECAM - Electronic Centralized Aircraft Monitoring
EDT - Eastern Daylight Time
EFIS - Electronic Flight Instrument System
EICAS - Engine Indicating and Crew Alerting System
ELT - Emergency Locator Transmitter
EMER(S) - Emergency
EMI - Electromagnetic Interference
EMS - Emergency Medical Service
ENG - Engine
ENGR - Engineer
ENRTE - En Route
EQUIP - Equipment
EROPS - Extended Range Operations
EST - Estimate, Estimation
EST - Eastern Standard Time

ETA - Estimated Time Of Arrival
ETD - Estimated Time Of Departure
ETOPS - Extended Range Twin Operations
EVAC (S,ED) - Evacuate/Evacuation
EVAL - Evaluate, Evaluation
EXAM - Examination
F - Fahrenheit
FA('S) - Flight Attendant
FAA - Federal Aviation Administration
FAC - Facility
FAF - Final Approach Fix
FAM - Federal Air Marshal
FAR(S) - Federal Aviation Regulation
FAX - Facsimile
FBO - Fixed-Base Operator
FCC - Federal Communications Commission
FCDU - Flight Control Data Concentrator
FCU - Flight Control Unit
FD - Flight Director
FE('S) - Flight Engineer
FGC - Flight Guidance Computer
FGS - Flight Guidance Unit
FIDO - Flight Inspection District Office
FL - Flight Level
FLC - Flight Crew
FLIP - Flight Information Publication
FLT - Flight
FM - Frequency Modulation
FMA - Flight Mode Annunciator
FMC - Flight Management Computer
FMGC - Flight Management Guidance Computer
FMGS - Flight Management Guidance System
FMS - Flight Management System
FO - First Officer
FOD - Foreign Object Damage
FPM - Feet Per Minute
FREQ(S) - Frequency
FSDO - Flight Standards District Office
FSS - Flight Service Station
FSS('S) - Flight Service Station Specialist
FT - Feet/Foot
FYI - For Your Information
GA - General Aviation
GADO - General Aviation District Office
GAR - Go Around
GC - Ground Control
GHZ - Gigahertz
GMT - Greenwich Mean Time

Acronyms According to NASA (Continued)

GND (S, ED, ING) - Ground
GND SPD - Ground Speed
GNS - Global Navigation System
GOV - Government
GPS - Global Positioning System
GPWS - Ground Proximity Warning System
GS - Glideslope (One Word)
HDG(S) - Heading
HDOF(S) - Handoff
HELI(S) - Helicopter
HF - High Frequency
HGT - Height
HIALS - High Intensity Approach Light System
HIRL - High Intensity Runway Lights
HORIZ(LY) - Horizontal
HQ - Headquarters
HR (S,LY) - Hour
HSI - Horizontal Situation Indicator
HUD - Head Up Display
HVY - Heavy
HWY - Highway
HYD - Hydraulic
HZ - Hertz
IAF - Initial Approach Fix
IAP - Instrument Approach Procedure
IAS - Indicated Air Speed
IATA - International Air Transport Association
IAW - In Accordance With
ICAO - International Civil Aviation Organization
ID - Identification
IDENT - Identify
IF - Intermediate Fix
IFF - Identification, Friend Or Foe
IFR - Instrument Flight Rules
IFSS - International Flight Service Station
ILS - Instrument Landing System
IMC - Instrument Meteorological Conditions
INBND - Inbound
INC - Incorporated
INFO - Information
INOP - Inoperative
INS - Inertial Navigation System
INST(S) - Instrument
INTERFAC - Inter-facility
INTERP - Interpretation

INTL - International
INTXN - Intersection
IOE - Initial Operating Experience
IRO - International Relief Officer
IRS/IRU - Inertial Reference System/Unit
ISDU - Inertial Navigation Display Unit
ISTR - Instruct, Instructor
KG - Kilogram
KHZ - Kilohertz
KIAS - Knots Indicated Airspeed
KM - Kilometers
KT(S) - Knot(S)
KW - Kilowatt
L/R - Left/Right (Directions)
LAT - Latitude
LB(S) - Pound
LC - Local Control
LCD - Liquid Crystal Display
LCL - Local
LED - Light Emitting Diode
LF - Low Frequency
LIRL - Low Intensity Runway Edge Lights
LLWAS - Low Level Wind Shear Alert System
LLWS - Low Level Wind Shear
LMM - Compass Locator At ILS Middle Marker
LNAV - Lateral Navigation
LNDG - Landing
LOA - Letter Of Agreement
LOC - Localizer
LOM - Compass Locator At ILS Outer Marker
LONG - Longitude
LORAN - Long Range Navigation
LTR - Letter
LTSS - Less Than Standard Separation
LWOC - Landing Without Clearance
M - Mach Number
MAG - Magnetic
MAINT - Maintenance
MALS - Medium Intensity Approach Lighting System
MALSF - Medium Intensity Approach Lighting System With Sequenced Flashers
MALSR - Medium Intensity Approach Lighting System With Runway Alignment Indicator Lights
MAP - Missed Approach Point
MAX - Maximum
MB - Millibars

MCA - Minimum Crossing Altitude
MCAS - Marine Corps Air Station
MCP - Mode Control Panel
MDA - Minimum Descent Altitude
MDT - Mountain Daylight Time
MEA - Minimum Enroute Altitude
MECH - Mechanic
MEL - Minimum Equipment List
METRO - Metropolitan
MF - Medium Frequency
MFDU - Multi Functional Display Unit
MGMNT - Management
MGR - Manager
MHZ - Megahertz
MI - Mile
MIKE, MIC - Microphone
MIL - Military
MIN(S) - Minute(S)
MIRL - Medium Intensity Runway Edge Lights
MISC - Miscellaneous
MLS - Microwave Landing System
MM - Middle Marker
MOA - Military Operating Area
MOCA - Minimum Obstruction Clearance Altitude
MSA - Minimum Safe Altitude
MSAW - Minimum Safe Altitude Warning
MSG - Message
MSL - Mean Sea Level
MST - Mountain Standard Time
MTR - Military Training Route
MUNI - Municipal
MVA - Minimum Vector Altitude
MVFR - Marginal Visual Flight Rules
N,S,E,W - North, South, East, West
NAS - Naval Air Station
NASA - National Aeronautics & Space Administration
NATL - National
NAV (S,ING) - Navigate, Navigation
NAVAID - Navigational Aid
NBND - Northbound
NDB - Nondirectional Radio Beacon
NDB/DME - NDB and DME (Co-located) B55
NFCT - Non Federal Control Tower
NM - Nautical Mile
NMAC - Near Midair Collision
NOAA - National Oceanic & Atmospheric Admin

NORAC - No Radio Contact
NORDO - No Radio
NOTAM - Notice To Airmen
NTSB - National Transportation Safety Board
NWS - National Weather Service
OAT - Outside Air Temperature
OJT - On-The-Job Training
OM - Outer Marker
ONS - Omega Navigation System
OP(S) - Operation(S)
OPDEV - Operational Deviation
OPERROR - Operational Error
OTS - Out Of Service
OVCST - Overcast
PA - Public Address
PAPI - Precision Approach Path Indicator
PAR - Precision Approach Radar
PAX - Passenger
PCA - Positive Control Area
PCL - Pilot Controlled Lighting
PCU - Power Control Unit
PDC - Pre Departure Clearance
PDT - Pacific Daylight Time
PF - Pilot Flying
PIC - Pilot In Command
PIREP(S) - Pilot Report
PLT (S,'S) - Pilot
PLTDEV - Pilot Deviation
PM - Post Meridiem
PNF - Pilot Not Flying
POS - Position
PRECIP - Precipitation
PROB(S) - Problem
PROC(S) - Procedure
PROP(S) - Propeller
PROX - Proximity
PST - Pacific Standard Time
PUB - Publication
PVT - Private
PWR - Power
QFE - Height Above Airport Elevation
QRH - Quick Reference Handbook
RA - Resolution Advisory
RAIL - Runway Alignment Indicator Lights
RAPCON - Radar Approach Control
RAT - Ram Air Turbine/Ram Air Temperature
RDMI - Radio Direction Magnetic Indicator
REF (S, ED, ING) - Reference
REG(S) - Regulation

Acronyms According to NASA (Continued)

REIL - Runway End Identifier Lights
RESTR - Restrict, Restricted, Restriction
RF - Radio Frequency
RFI - Radio Frequency Interference
RMI - Radio Magnetic Indicator
RNAV - Area Navigation
RPM - Revolutions Per Minute
RTE - Route
RTO - Rejected Takeoff
RVR - Runway Visual Range
RVV - Runway Visibility Value
RWY(S) - Runway(s)
SBND - Southbound
SELCAL - Selective Calling
SFL - Sequence Flashing Lights
SID - Standard Instrument Departure
SIGMET - Significant Meteorological Information
SIT - Situation
SL - Sea Level
SM - Statute Mile
SO('S) - Second Officer
SOP - Standard Operating Procedure
SPD (S,ING) - Speed
SPEC(S) - Specification
STAB - Stabilizer
STAR - Standard Terminal Arrival Route
STD - Standard
STOL - Short Takeoff and Landing
SUPVR(S) - Supervisor
SVC(S) - Service
SVFR - Special Visual Flight Rules
SYS - System
TA - Traffic Advisory
TACAN - Tactical Air Navigation Aid
TAS - True Air Speed
TCA - Terminal Control Area
TCAS - Traffic Alert and Collision Avoidance System
TDZ - Touchdown Zone
TELCO - Telephone Company
TEMP(S) - Temperature
TFC - Traffic
TKOF(S) - Takeoff
TOC - Top Of Climb
TOD - Top Of Descent
TOGW - Takeoff Gross Weight
TR - VFR Low Altitude Training Routes

TRACON - Terminal Radar Approach Control Facility
TRNG - Training
TRSA - Terminal Radar Service Area
TSTM(S) - Thunderstorm
TURB - Turbulence
TWR(S) - Tower
TXWY - Taxiway
UFO - Unidentified Flying Object
UHF - Ultra High Frequency
UNAUTH - Unauthorized
USA - U S Army
USAF - U S Air Force
USCG - U S Coast Guard
USMC - U S Marine Corps
USN - U S Navy
UTC - Universal Time Constant (Zulu/GMT)
VASI - Visual Approach Slope Indicator
VERT(LY) - Vertical
VFR - Visual Flight Rules
VHF - Very High Frequency
VIS - Visibility
VLF - Very Low Frequency
VMC - Visual Meteorological Conditions
VNAV - Vertical Navigation
VOR - VFR Omni-Directional Radio Range
VOR/DME - VOR and DME (Co-located)
VORTAC - VOR and TACAN (Co-Located)
VR - VFR Military Training Routes
VSTOL - Vertical/Short Takeoff and Landing
WAC - World Aeronautical Chart
WBND - Westbound
WK (S,LY) - Week
WT(S) - Weight
WX - Weather
XCOUNTRY - Cross Country
XING - Crossing
XMISSION - Transmission
XMIT (S,TING) - Transmit
XPONDER - Transponder
XWIND - Crosswind
Z - Coordinated Universal Time, same GMT

Aircraft Types According to NASA

This is the list of aircraft types that have been used in Part 91 Personal or Training flights. This is not an exhaustive list, so if you see something missing, please drop me an email.

A109 All Series
Aero Commander 500 Series
Aero Commander 520 Series
Aero Commander 680 Series
Aero Commander 685
Aero Commander 695
Aero Vodochody Undiff/OM
Aeronca Champion
Aircoupe A2
Airliner 99
Albatros (L39)
Alon, Inc Undiff/OM
Amateur (Home) Built
Any Unknown or Unlisted Acft Mfg
Any Unknown or Unlisted Helicopter
Apache/Apache Longbow (AH-64)
AS 355 Twinstar
AV8B Harrier II
AV-8B Harrier II
B1 Lancer
B707 Undiff/OM
B717
B737-400
B747 Undiff/OM
B777-200
BAe 125 Series 800
BAE Harrier/Sea Harrier
Balloon
Baron 55/Cochise
Baron 58/58TC
Beaver DHC-2
Beech 1900
Beech F90
Beechcraft King Air Undiff/OM
Beechcraft Single Piston Undiff/OM
Beechcraft Twin Piston Undiff/OM
Beechcraft Twin Turboprop or Jet Beechcraft
Beechjet 400
Bell 47
Bell Helicopter Textron Undiff/OM
Bellanca Aircraft Corp Undiff/OM
Bird Dog 305/321
Boeing Business Jet (BBJ 1/2/3)
Bombardier Learjet Undiff/OM
Bombardier/Canadair Undiff/OM
Bonanza 33
Bonanza 35
Bonanza 36

Brasilia EMB-120 All Series
British Aerospace Undiff/OM
Buckeye (T-2)
Buffalo DHC-5
C-12 Huron
C17
Cadet Mark 10
Caravan 208A
Caravan 208B
Cardinal 177/177RG
Cessna 120
Cessna 140
Cessna 150
Cessna 152
Cessna 170
Cessna 180 Skywagon
Cessna 195
Cessna 210 Centurion / Turbo 210C, 210D
Cessna 310/T310C
Cessna 335
Cessna 336 Skymaster
Cessna 337 Super Skymaster
Cessna 340/340A
Cessna 400
Cessna 401
Cessna 402/402C/B379
Cessna 404 Titan
Cessna 411
Cessna 425 Corsair
Cessna 425/441 Conquest I/Conquest II
Cessna Aircraft Undiff/OM
Cessna Citation Undiff/OM
Cessna Citation Mustang (C510)
Cessna Citation Undiff/OM
Cessna Single Piston Undiff/OM
Cessna Single Turboprop Undiff/OM
Cessna Stationair/Turbo Stationair 6
Cessna Stationair/Turbo Stationair 7/8
Cessna Super Skywagon/Super Skylane
Cessna T-37 (Tweet)/A-37 (Dragonfly)
Cessna Twin Piston Undiff/OM
Cessna Twin Turboprop Undiff/OM
Challenger 300
Challenger CL600
Challenger CL601
Challenger CL603/603a
Challenger CL604
Champion Citabria 7ECA

Aircraft Types According to NASA (Continued)

Champion Citabria Undifferentiated
Chancellor 414A & C414
Cheetah, Tiger, Traveler AA5 Series
Chinook (CH-47)
Christen A-1 Huskey
Christen Eagle II
Christen/Pitts Undiff/OM
Cirrus (all models)
Citation Excel (C560XL)
Citation I (C500)
Citation I/SP (C501)
Citation II S2/Bravo (C550)
Citation II/SP (C551)
Citation III, VI, VII (C650)
Citation V/Ultra/Encore (C560)
Citation X (C750)
Citationjet (C525/C526) - CJ I/II/III/IV
Commander 112/A/B/TC
Commander 112A
Commander 112TC
Commander 114/A/B/TC
Commander 200
Commander 900
Commander Prop Jet Undiff/OM
Commercial Fixed Wing
Convair 240/340 Liner/Convertible
Convair 880
Cougar F9F
Cruisemaster 14-13
CV 580
DA20 Undifferentiated
DA20-A1 Katana
DA20-C1 Eclipse
DA40 Diamond Star
DA42 Twin Star
Darter 100/150
Dash 8 Series Undiff/OM
DC-10 Undiff/OM
DC-3/Dakota/Skytrain
DC-9 Undiff/OM
De Havilland Canada Undiff/OM
Decathlon 8KCAB
Diamond Aircraft Undiff/OM
Duchess 76
Duke 60
E-3 Sentry (AWACS)
Eagle (F-15)
Eclipse 500
Electra L-188
Embraer Legacy 450/500
Embraer Undiff/OM

Enstrom Helicopter 280 Shark
Eurocopter AS 350/355/EC130
Eurocopter AS 365 Dauphin
Experimental
Experimental; Bell Helicopter 222
Extra 200/300 Series
F-28 Enstrom Helicopter
Fairchild Swearingen Undiff/OM
Falcon 10/100
Falcon 20FJF/20C/20D/20E/20F
Falcon 50
Falcon 900
Fighter
Fighting Falcon F16
Fokker 100
Fokker 50/60
Galaxy (C5A)
Global 5000 (Bombardier)
Golden Eagle 421
Goose/Super Goose G-21
Grumman American Undiff/OM
Grumman Corp Undiff/OM
Gulfstream G200 (IAI 1126 Galaxy)
Gulfstream I (Large Turboprop)
Gulfstream II (G1159)
Gulfstream III (G1159A)
Gulfstream IV/G350/G450
Gulfstream V/G500/G550
Hawker Horizon (Raytheon)
Heavy Transport, Low Wing, 4 Turbojet Eng
Helicopter
Hercules (C-130)
Hiller Helicopter, Undiff/OM
Hornet (F-18)
HS 125 Series
HS 125 Series 600
HS 125 Series 700
IAI1123 Westwind
IAI1124/1124A Westwind
IAI1125 (Astra)
Intruder (A6)
Israel Aircraft Undiff/OM
J3 Cub
Jet Ranger All Series Undiff/OM
Jet Ranger III
Jet/Long Ranger/206
Jetstar 1329 (C140)
Jetstream 32
Jetstream Series Commuter Aircraft
King Air 100 A/B
King Air C90 E90

Kiowa Warrior
Kiowa/Kiowa Warrior/Combat Scout
LA-250 (Renegade/Seawolf)
LA-270 (Turbo Renegade/Sea Fury)
LA-4 A/B Buccaneer
LA-4-200 Buccaneer
Lake Aircraft Undiff/OM
Lancair 360
Lancair Columbia
Lancair IV/IVP
Lancair Legacy
Lancair Undifferentiated
Lark
Learjet 24
Learjet 25
Learjet 29
Learjet 31
Learjet 35
Learjet 36
Learjet 55
Learjet 60
Light Sport Aircraft
Light Transport
Light Transport, Low Wing, 2 Turbojet Eng
Light Transport, Low Wing, 2 Turbrop Eng
Lockheed Corp Undiff/OM
Luscombe (Silvaire) Undiff/OM
Luscombe Model 8/Luscombe 50
M-20 A Scotsman
M-20 B/C Ranger
M-20 D Master
M-20 E Super 21
M-20 F Executive 21
M-20 G Statesman
M-20 J (201)/Allegro
M-20 K (231)/Encore
M-20 L
M-20 M Bravo
M-20 R Ovation
M-20 Series Undiff/OM
M-20 TN Acclaim
M-22 Mustang
M-30
M-4 Rocket
M-5
M-6
M-7
Maule Aircraft Corp Undiff/OM
McDonnell Douglas Undiff/OM
MD Helicopter 500/C/D/E/L
MD-500MG
Med Lrg Transport, Low Wing, 2 jet Eng

Med Transport, High Wing, 2 prop Eng
Med Transport, Low Wing, 2 Tjet Eng
Mentor/Turbo Mentor (T-34)
Merlin III
Military
Military Trainer
Military Transport
Mitsubishi Aircraft Undiff/OM
Model 269A/300/Osage
Mooney Aircraft Undiff/OM
MU-2
MU-2 Undiff/OM
MU-300 Diamond 1/1A
Musketeer 23
Mustang (P51)
Navion
Navion Aircraft Corp Undiff/OM
Nighthawk (F117) Stealth Fighter
No Aircraft
Northrop Corp Undiff/OM
Orion (P3)
Other
P180 Avanti
PA-18/19 Super Cub
PA-20 Pacer/PA-22 Tri-Pacer
PA-23 Apache/Geronimo Apache
PA-23-250 Aztec
PA-23-250 Turbo Aztec
PA-24 Comanche
PA-24 Turbo Comanche
PA-25 Pawnee
PA-28 Cherokee/Archer/Dakota/Warrior
PA-28R Cherokee Arrow All Series
PA-30 Twin Comanche
PA-31 Navajo/Chieftan/Mojave/T1040
PA-31P Navajo P
PA-31T Cheyenne I
PA-31T Cheyenne II
PA-31-X2 Cheyenne XL
PA-32 Cherokee Six/Lance/Saratoga/6X
PA-34 Seneca Undifferentiated
PA-34-200 Seneca I
PA-34-200T Turbo Seneca II
PA-34-220T Turbo Seneca III
PA-36 Pawnee Brave
PA-38 Tomahawk
PA-42 Cheyenne II/IIIA
PA-42 Cheyenne IIA
PA-44 Seminole/Turbo Seminole
PA-46 Malibu Meridian
PA-46 Malibu/Malibu Mirage/Malibu Matrix
PA-60 600 Aerostar

Undiff/OM = Undifferentiated or Other Model, means a model other than already recognized

PA-60 601/601P Aerostar
PA-60 602 Aerostar
PA-60 700P
PC-12
Piper Aircraft Corp Undiff/OM
Piper Single Undiff/OM
Piper Twin Piston Undiff/OM
Piper Twin Turboprop Undiff/OM
Premier 1
Queen Air 65/70 (Seminole)
Rallye 180T/180T-D/180TS
Rallye Minerva MS-984
Rangemaster (Navion)
Robinson Helicopter, Undiff/OM
Robinson R22
Robinson R44
Rockwell Aero Commander Single
Rockwell Aero Commander Twin Turbprop
Rockwell North American Civil Twin Jet
Rockwell North American Undiff/OM
RV-10
RV-4
RV-6
RV-7
RV-8
S-1 All Series
S-2 All Series
S-70/UH-60 (Black Hawk/Sea Hawk/Pave
          Hawk/Knight Hawk/Jay Hawk)
S-76/S-76 Mark II
SA 341/342 Gazelle
SA-226 TC Metro II
SA-227 AC Metro III
Sabreliner 265
Sabreliner 60
Sail Plane
Scout 8GCBC
Seaplane or Amphibian
SF 340A
Shooting Star (T-33)
Shorts SD-330
Sierra 24
Sikorsky Helicopter Undiff/OM
Skipper 77
Skyhawk (A4)
Skyhawk 172/Cutlass 172
Skylane 182/RG Turbo Skylane/RG
Skylark 175
Skynight 320
Skywagon 185
Small Acft, High Wing, 1 Eng, Fixed Gear

Small Acft, High Wing, 1 Eng, Retract Gear
Small Acft, Low Wing, 1 Eng, Fixed Gear
Small Acft, Low Wing, 1 Eng, Retract Gear
Small Acft, Low Wing, 2 Eng, Retract Gear
Small Transport
Small Transport, Low Wing, 2 Recip Eng
Small Transport, Low Wing, 2 Turbojet Eng
Small Transport, Low Wing, 2 Turboprop Eng
Socata (Aerospatiale), Undiff/OM
Sport 19
SR20
SR22
Stagger Wing 17
Starlifter (C141)
Starship Model 2000
Stearman
Stratofortress (B-52)
Stratoliner (C-135)/Stratotanker (KC-135)
Stratotanker 135
Sundowner 23
Super Hercules (C130J)
Super King Air 200
Super King Air 300
Super King Air 350
T-1020
T45 (or T2C) Goshawk
T6A Texan II / Harvard II (Raytheon)
Talon (T38)
Tampico TB-9
TBM 700/TBM 850
Texan T6/Harvard (Antique)
Thunderbolt II (Warthog A-10)
Tiger (F11)
Tobago TB-10C
Tomcat (F14)
Travelair 95
Trinidad TB-20
Trinidad TB-21
Trojan (T28)
Turbo Commander 690 Series
Turbo Commander 840 Series (Jetprop)
Twin Beech 18
Twin Bonanza 50
Twin Navion
Twin Otter DHC-6
UH-12E/E4
Ultralight
Viking
Viking/Turbo-Viking 17-30/31
Widgeon G-44
Yankee AA1

Undiff/OM = Undifferentiated or Other Model, means a model other than already recognized

"Real knowledge is to know the extent of one's ignorance."
— *Confucius*

Appendix

Personal Minimums Checklist
ADAPTATION REPRINT OF FAA P-8740-55 AFS-810(1996)

PILOT

AIRCRAFT

EN**V**IRONMENT

EXTERNAL
PRESSURES

Your Personal Minimums Checklist
O An easy-to-use, personal tool, tailored to your level of skill, knowledge & ability.
O Helps you control and manage risk by identifying even subtle risk factors
O Lets you fly with less stress and less risk.

Practice "Conservatism Without Guilt"
Each item provides you with either a space to complete a personal minimum or a checklist item to think about. Spend some quiet time completing each blank & consider other items that apply to your personal minimums. Give yourself permission to choose higher minimums than those specified in the regulations, aircraft flight manuals, or other rules.

How to Use Your Checklist
Use this checklist just as you would one for your aircraft. Carry the checklist in your flight kit. Use it at home as you start planning a flight and again just before you make your final decision to fly. Photocopy the next page (front & back) and carry extras in your flight bag. Be wary if you have an item that's marginal in any single risk factor category. But if you have items in more than one category, you may be headed for trouble.

If you have marginal items in two or more risk factors/ categories, don't go!
Periodically review and revise your personal minimums checklist as your personal circumstances change, such as your proficiency, recency, or training. You should never make your minimums less restrictive unless a significant positive event has occurred. However, it is okay to make your minimums more restrictive at any time. Never make your minimums less restrictive when you are planning a specific flight, or else external pressures will influence you.

PILOT

Experience/Recency

Takeoffs/Landings	____In the last ____days
Hours in make/model	____In the last ____days
Instrument approaches (simulated or actual)	____In the last ____days
Instrument flight hours (simulated or actual)	____In the last ____days
Terrain and airspace	____Familiar?

Physical Condition

Illnesses, none in the last ____days

Medication/Drugs, none in ____days

Stressful Event, none in ____days

Alcohol, none in the last ____In the last 24hrs

Fatigue: hours of sleep ____In the last 24hrs

Eating/Nourishment/Water ____hours ago

_____

_____

_____

_____

_____

Thanks to:

FAA Aviation Safety Program
The Ohio State University
King Schools

AIRCRAFT

Fuel Reserves

VFR Day ____ hours

Night ____ hours

IFR Day ____ hours

Night ____ hours

Experience in type

Takeoffs/Landings ____ In the last

(in aircraft type) ____ days

Aircraft Performance

Consider the following:

- Gross weight ____
- Load distribution ____
- Density Altitude ____
- Performance Charts ____

Ensure you have a margin of safety

Aircraft Equipment

Avionics/GPS, familiar with ____

Autopilot, familiar with ____

COM/NAV, appropriate ____

Charts, current & adequate ____

Clothing, suitable for flight ____

Survival gear, suitable for flight ____

Required Documents (ARROW) ____

Required Inspections (AVIATE) ____

Required Equipment (§91.205) ____

Other ____

_____

_____

_____

_____

_____

EN**V**IRONMENT

Airport Conditions

Crosswind, Departure	_____	% max POH
Crosswind, Arrival	_____	% max POH
Runway length, Departure	_____	% over POH
Runway length, Arrival	_____	% over POH

Weather

Forecast, not more than	_____	Hours old
Icing conditions, familiar	_____	

Weather for VFR

Ceiling	Day	_____	feet
	Night	_____	feet
Visibility	Day	_____	miles
	Night	_____	miles

Weather for IFR

Precision Approaches

Ceiling	_____	ft above min
Visibility	_____	mi above min

Non-Precision Approaches

Ceiling	_____	ft above min
Visibility	_____	mi above min

Missed Approaches

No more than	_____	before divert

Takeoff Minimums

Ceiling	_____	feet
Visibility	_____	miles

_____

_____

_____

_____

_____

_____

EXTERNAL PRESSURES

Trip Planning
Allowance for delays, _____ minutes

Diversion/Cancellation Alternate Plans
- ✓ Notification of person(s) you are meeting.
- ✓ Passengers briefed on diversion/cancellation plans and alternates.
- ✓ Modification or cancellation of car rental, restaurant, or hotel reservations.
- ✓ Alternate transportation (air/car/etc)

Personal Equipment
- ✓ Credit card & telephone numbers available for alternate plans.
- ✓ Appropriate clothing or personal needs (eyewear, medication…) in the event of unexpected stay.

Importance of Trip
The more important the trip, the more tendency there is to compromise your personal minimums, and the more important it becomes to have alternate plans.

For More Information, Contact:

Darren Smith, ATP, CFII/MEI
Certificated Flight Instructor
www.cfidarren.com

7-Day Instrument Rating Training

Structured, Efficient, & Cost Effective:

O Get 7 days of <u>individualized experience</u> for Your Training Investment.

O <u>Gain real confidence</u> working the IFR system with airline style routes.

O <u>Learn real world techniques</u> from an experienced Instructor (CFII)

O Build IFR skills in your aircraft - in a format convenient to your schedule.

Want to finish your IFR Rating in 7 days?

If you're interested in getting your instrument in 7 days, this is the program for you. There are no gimmicks to this, it's hard work, and requires your full concentration. But when you're finished, you'll have gained solid experience in the real world of IFR.

Don't spend 9-12 months and $7,000 to $10,000 on your instrument rating! Condensed training experiences will not only save you money, but the intensity guarantees that the lessons last a lifetime. Your training is accelerated and less time is spent reviewing the last lesson... a real money saver. None of the other accelerated programs provide the comprehensive, high quality learning materials: the Oral Exam Prep Kit and the Instrument Rating Checkride Reviewer.

The three-day IFR Adventure is an integral part of the seven day IFR Rating and guarantees a unique training experience. We integrate the IFR Adventure into the course not only to meet certain instrument rating requirements, but also to serve as a real world capstone experience which increases your confidence in the IFR system.

What if you want a slower pace than a 7 day instrument rating training course?   A 10-day program is available at a slightly higher cost.

Key Features:

O The program includes up to 56 hours of one-on-one ground & flight instruction.

O You will receive <u>at least</u> 30 hours of one-on-one flight instruction on some of the most challenging instrument approaches in the South East. You'll fly at least 25 approaches during the program, many with SID's STAR's and holding patterns. You'll be astonished at how much you will learn.

O When you are not in the air, you will learn techniques that will simplify otherwise complex procedures such as procedure turns, holding pattern entries and many others.

O Includes a 3 day IFR Adventure which adds up to a true flying adventure that will make you a more knowledgeable and confident pilot... plus it's a whole lot of fun!

O You are PIC for the entire program receiving PIC credit in your logbook for 100% of the flight time.

O We know your aircraft—we've got time virtually all aircraft & helicopters and avionics configurations.

6 Reasons to Choose This Program:

1. This is a quick, efficient, structured training program to get you through this training with minimum pain, maximum quality.
2. We constantly evaluate our competitors to ensure that our program provides the highest quality at the most reasonable cost in the country... compare for yourself. We're not beat by anyone.
3. You are PIC for the entire program receiving PIC credit in your logbook for 100% of the flight time.
4. Safety: techniques for safe instrument flight are emphasized by your instructor.
5. Personal attention is provided as you progress through your training program. You'll never wonder about your progress. You will never fall through the cracks .
6. The chief instructor has been a teacher since 1996, is a Master Instructor (NAFI), Advanced Ground Instructor rated (FAA), a Gold Seal Certificated Flight Instructor (FAA), an Aviation Safety Counselor (FAA), and a former airline pilot. Your instructor is a highly qualified ATP-rated, FAA Gold Seal, NAFI Master instructor with 100% pass rate. None of the other local providers use an instructor of this calibre.

Prerequisites for Instrument Rating:

You'll be ready for a checkride immediately upon completion if you have:
○ a passing score on your instrument written,
○ at least 50 hours PIC X/C & at least 40 hours of instrument time,
○ and meet PTS requirements

Those that don't meet these requirements will receive instruction at reduced rate. This can be completed before or after the trip. What if you want a slower pace than a 7 day instrument rating training course? A 10-day program is available at a slightly higher cost.

Availability:

Call for scheduling. Includes: All flight and ground instruction, over 56 hours combined. Orientation ground package.

Not Included: Aircraft or anything related to the aircraft (Fuel, Oil, Insurance, Rental, Gov Fees, Repair, Etc), Meals, Ground Transportation & Lodging for you & your instructor, entertainment or any personal expenses you might encounter. You must supply your own aircraft, oil & fuel.

Participant Comments:

"You have a 'teaching way' about you and its very effective." Dave C
"You really have this down to a science." Alan D
*"Thank you for the many flights of stressing good flying habits.
Its now paying off in my Air Force career."* Mark S
*"My training was second to none. My skills are consistently
complimented by other flight instructors I have flown with"* Tim N

www.ifrnow.com

South East IFR Adventure
In Your Aircraft
Our Practice Area is a 2,000 mile Cross Country Training Adventure!

Intense 3-day IFR Confidence Builder

O Get More Individualized Experience For Your Training Investment.
O Gain real confidence working the IFR system with airline style routes.
O Learn Real World Techniques from an experienced Instructor (CFII)
O Finish your instrument rating or IPC & build IFR skills in your aircraft.
O We can start your IFR adventure anyplace and customize it to your location.
O Get more than current, get proficient.

Want a real IFR workout?

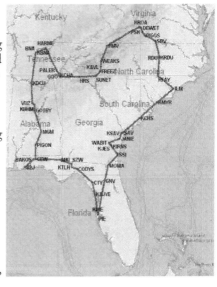

If you're interested in finishing your instrument rating or gaining solid experience in the real world of IFR, here's a unique opportunity for an accelerated program for aircraft owners that is completed in **3 days**.

This Southeast Trip is a flying adventure, traveling up the east coast, down the Blue Ridge Mountain chain to the Great Smoky Mountain, through the heartland, and back down through the Mississippi Valley. You will gain the experience of flying over 2,000 miles and over 20 flight hours. Upon our return, you'll receive your IPC or endorsement for the check-ride. In addition, you'll enjoy spectacular scenery, gain valuable experience by training away from your local airport and receive professional instruction in a variety of flight conditions.

This training experience gives you the confidence you need to really use the IFR system. You'll operate in the environment like a professional by focusing on the practical aspects of instrument flight. You will also get a chance to really learn some of the most challenging instrument approaches in the country, performing them like the professionals.

Key Features:

- Your orientation includes ground instruction, briefings, flight planning.
- You will receive over 20 hours of one-on-one flight instruction on some of the most challenging instrument approaches in the Southeast.
- When you are not in the air, you will learn techniques that will simplify otherwise complex procedures such as procedure turns, holding pattern entries and many others.
- You'll receive over 10 hours of ground instruction during the course of the program... you will be confident you can pass your checkride.
- If instrument rated, you will receive your IPC immediately upon return. Instrument rating completion students will typically take their instrument checkride immediately upon returning.
- In all, you complete **at least** 10 approaches, many with SID's, STAR's, & holding.
- You'll be astonished at how much you will learn in this total immersion experience.
- Aircraft owners: this is the ultimate insurance checkout if you need it.
- All of this adds up to a true flying adventure that will make you a more knowledgeable and confident pilot...plus it's a whole lot of fun!
- We know your aircraft—we've got time virtually all aircraft & helicopters and avionics configurations.

Prerequisites for Instrument Rating:

You'll be ready for an IPC or IFR check-ride immediately upon return if you have:

- a passing score on your instrument written,
- at least 50 hours PIC X/C & at least 40 hours of instrument time,
- and meet PTS requirements

Those that don't meet these requirements will receive instruction at reduced rate. This can be completed before or after the trip.

Availability:

This program starts every other Friday. Call for scheduling. Other routes and schedules are available for this highly individualized program.

Includes: All flight and ground instruction, over 35 hours combined. Orientation ground package including Checkride Review Guide

Not Included: Aircraft or anything related to the aircraft (Fuel, Oil, Insurance, Rental, Gov Fees, Repair, Etc), Meals, Ground Transportation & Lodging for you & your instructor, entertainment or any personal expenses you might encounter. You must supply your own aircraft, oil & fuel.

www.ifradventure.com

Introducing...

One of the most comprehensive
Flight Training websites available

Resources for all pilots:

- Articles on current practices and techniques to help you fly safely (in the Reading section)
- Links to other websites.
- Download section.
- FAA Safety Publications, Manuals, Practical Test Standards, and Training Guides.
- Free question & answer on difficult aviation topics, answered by an expert.
- An online store to purchase training products for your rating.
- Information on aviation ground schools, including syllabus, schedule, and enrollment info.
- Information resources for getting back into flying, including information & structure of Flight Reviews (BFR) and Instrument Proficiency Checks (IPC).
- An extensive graphical & textual weather products page with thumbnail views of all the current weather.
- Human Factors for pro pilots

Resources for helicopter pilots:

- Complete syllabus online including a maneuvers checklist.
- Reading library, articles, and information on the various helicopter ratings.
- Helicopter Lesson Plans for helicopter students.

Resources for multi-engine pilots:

- Complete syllabus online including a maneuvers checklist.

www.cfidarren.com

Responsibility & Authority of the PIC (§91.3)

The PIC is directly responsible for and the final authority in determining the airworthiness and operation of the aircraft. The PIC may deviate from any FAR to meet the requirements of an emergency. If the PIC deviates from and FAR, he or she shall, if requested, send a written report of the deviation to the Administrator.

Other Products by Darren Smith

Visi-Hold™ - *Know Instantly*

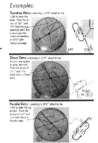

Examples:

Never wonder about holding entries again! Works with standard holds and non-standard holds (left turns). The Visi-Hold™ package comes complete with Visi-Hold™ template, directions, and two articles on holds: All About Holding and Holding Simplified. You'll pay no less than $14.95 for a complicated sliderule holding pattern calculator made by ASA. That's not even including shipping! Those of you who know what real IFR is like know that you can't fool around with a sliderule while the airplane is bouncing around. Instead, get the original Visi-Hold™, helping pilots know the holding pattern entry since 2000. Price: $10

Guaranteed Pass Helicopter Flash Cards

This package includes 240 easy to read, soft yellow cards -- not flimsy paper -- which will help you pass your FAA written and oral (checkride) helicopter exams. Card size approximately: 4.25" x 2.75" - a stack of cards approximately 2" high. Includes all helicopter subjects. Price: $25

Visi-Plotter™ - Simply the Best Flight Planning Plotter Made

This is the only VFR plotter invented by a CFI for pilots. It includes innovative features that provides temperature conversion, flight planning scratch pad area, and a no-mistakes course protractor that even beginners won't be confused by. It provides scales for sectional & WAC charts, and it even has inches & MM measurements. Price $15

The Most Accurate

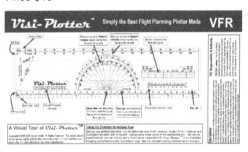

The Visi-Plotter navigational plotter is created from a calibrated hot stamp. It is the most accurate way to create a plotter. No other plotter on the market uses this production method because its more expensive than the silk screen method used by every other manufacturer.

Pilot's Rules of Thumb™ - the ultimate VFR/IFR Checklist

The ultimate checklist that every pilot needs. Ten years in development, this is a product that pilots of all levels of experience can immediately use. This tool covers 30 normal and non-normal situations and has 9 special tools that you'll use on every flight.   This high-quality plastic ruler/checklist measures approximately 3.75" x 9". Click the picture to see a larger picture of this tool or click the link for more information. Price: $4

Online Ordering - Free Shipping
www.cfidarren.com

Instrument Rating Checkride Reviewer

Finally, instrument rating help! The best seller review guide is designed to help you to get through the Instrument Checkride. Includes a special offer for <u>Visi-Hold</u>™ (see other side) as a bonus. This package can be used as a self study guide or by flight instructors to provide IPC/Checkride preparation. Designed to fit in your flight bag, size: 6" x 9" Price: $25

Getting the Most from Your Flight Training

This is the essential guide to becoming a better pilot, paying the least, getting the most, and finishing as quickly as possible. Includes sections on Becoming a Better Pilot, Ground & Flight Instruction Tips, and Earning Certificates & Ratings. Designed to fit in your flight bag, size: 6" x 9" Price: v$15

Pilot's Radio Communications Guide

This review guide is designed as a quick reference guide or radio communications training self study guide. This covers VFR & IFR radio communications. Build your confidence by knowing what to say and when. Designed to fit in your flight bag, size: 6" x 9" Price: $15

Learning IFR Enroute Charts

This 40 page guide helps the Flight Instructor or Instrument Students with IFR Enroute Symbology. It uses a unique IFR Chart Extract to teach symbology. It includes all symbology you need to know for your Instrument checkride or Instrument Proficiency Check. As a bonus chapter, Instrument Approach Procedure (plate) symbology is also included. All of which you need to know prior to your checkride. Price: $10

I've Screwed Up! - Now What?

Practical advice and tips using the NASA form when you've violated the FARs. This 48 page guide will walk you step by step through filing a NASA safety report. It will tell you the techniques and traps to submit a good report AND keep your pilot certificate unblemished. Price: $15.

Safer Approaches

Safer Approaches will teach you how to conduct Instrument Approach Procedures to a higher standard of safety and precision. You will learn:
- Four Fundamentals of Safe Approaches,
- How to virtually eliminate possibility of Controlled Flight Into Terrain,
- How to perform a Constant Angle Non-Precision Approach (CANPA),
- How to calculate a Visual Descent Point (VDP),
- How to practice building your flying precision.

Includes the Stabilized Approach Descent Rate Table, a plastic, kneeboard sized IFR tool that will eliminate the mental math applying these techniques during your IFR flying. 14pp. Price: $8

Winter Flying (PocketLearning)

Quick tips & techniques so you can get the most out of your winter flying - safely. Includes information on Winter Preflight, Induction Icing, Carb Icing, Airframe Icing, Tail Stalls, Hypothermia Strategies for Reducing the Risk, Winter Survival Kit, Aeronautical Decision Making, and the Personal Minimums Checklist. Size: 5" x 8" Price: $8

Online Ordering – Free Shipping
www.cfidarren.com

Made in the USA
Middletown, DE
31 December 2021

57235585R00031